to my Abby

AT THE PIANO
BY
MORTON GOULD

Edited by Joseph Prostakoff

Contents

G. SCHIRMER, Inc.

DISTRIBUTED BY

HAL•LEONARD®
CORPORATION

7777 W. BLUEMOUND RD. P.O. BOX 13819 MILWAUKEE, WI 53213

AT THE PIANO - Book II

Abby's Song

MORTON GOULD

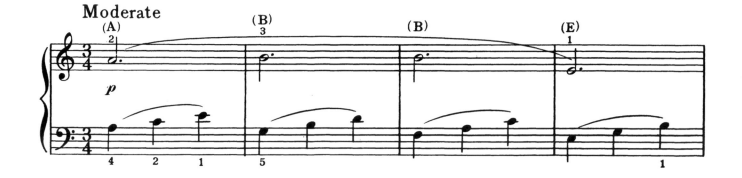

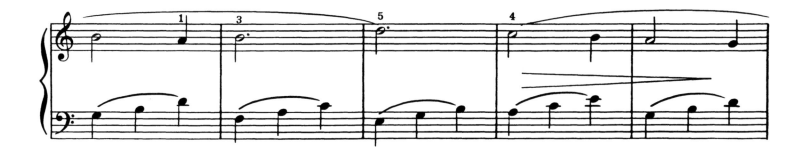

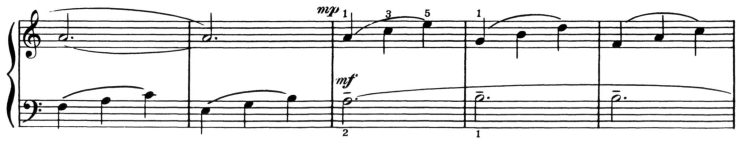

bring out melody

9631-15

Pastorale

With flowing movement

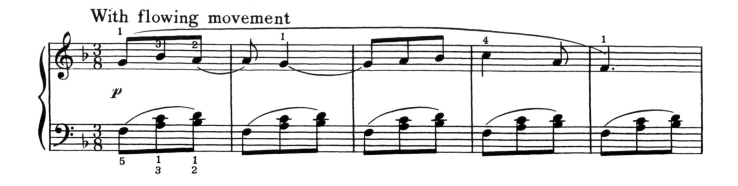

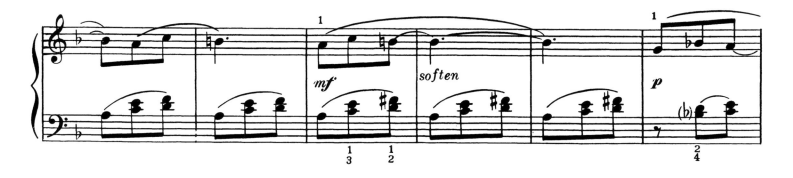

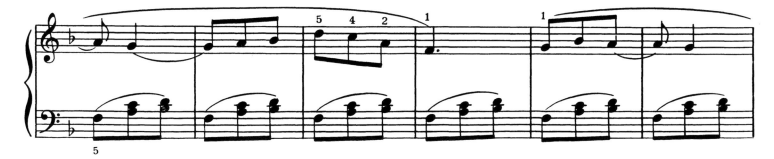

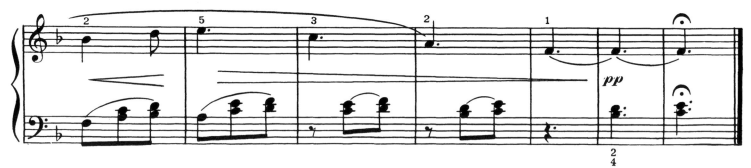

Waltz

Slowly and sweetly

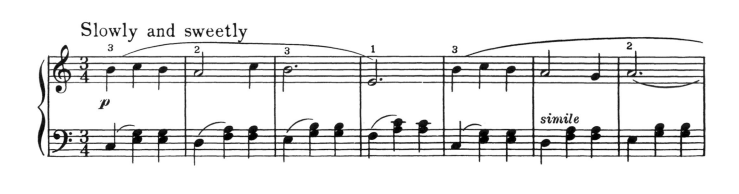

A Rough Game

Fast and brisk

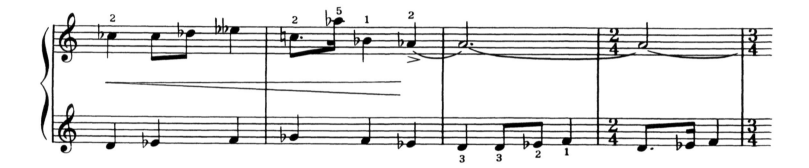

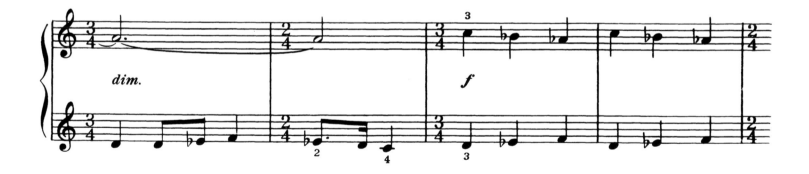

Wishing

Slowly and simply, with feeling

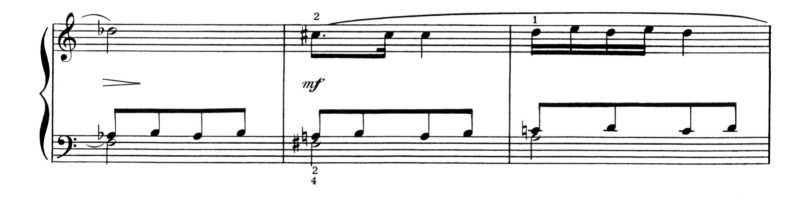

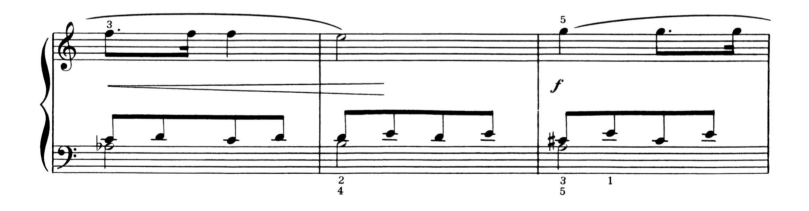

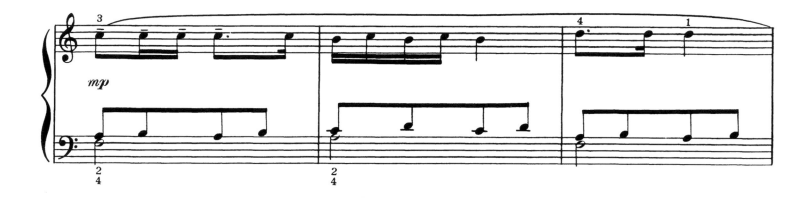

Rocking

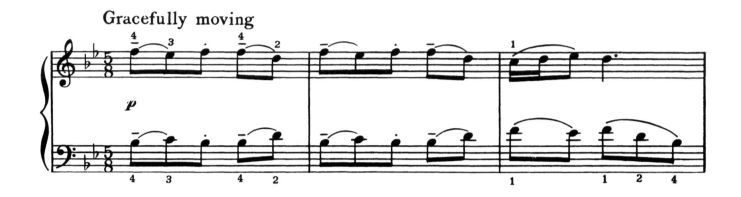

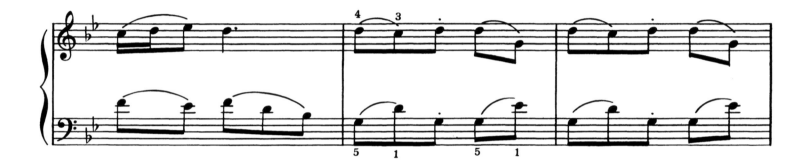

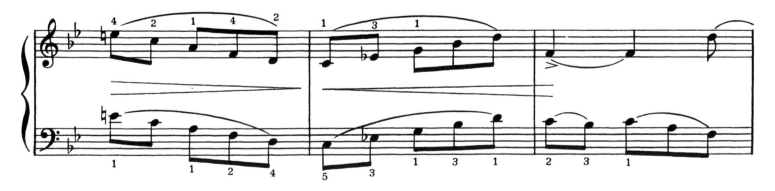

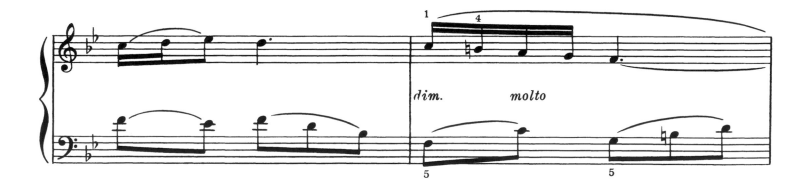

A Carol

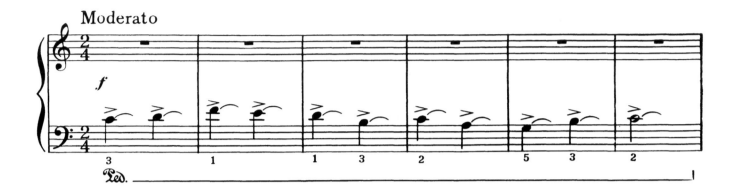

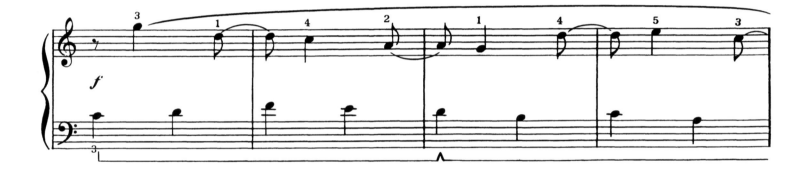

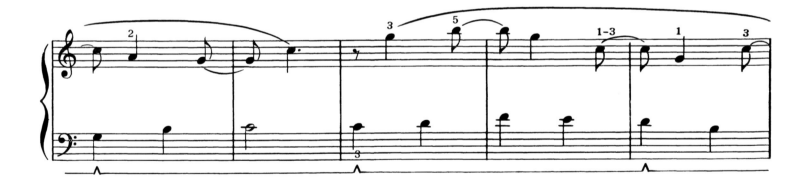

9631-15

A Special Special

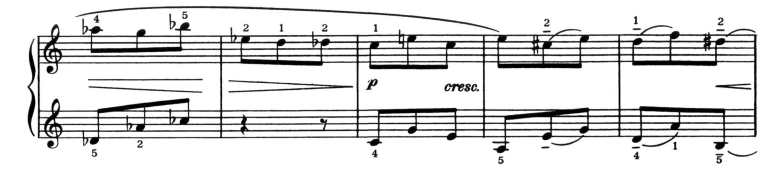

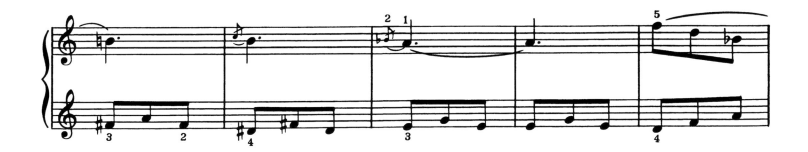

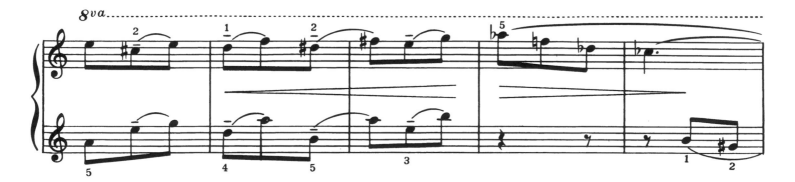

9631-15

Four Plus Five